Whizzy SCIENCE

Make it Zoom!

Written by:
Anna Claybourne

Illustrated by:
Kimberley Scott and Venetia Dean

Published in paperback in 2014 by Wayland
Copyright © Wayland 2014

Wayland
338 Euston Road
London NW1 3BH

Wayland Australia
Hachette Children's Books
Level 17/207
Kent Street
Sydney, NSW 2000

Senior Editor: Julia Adams
Designer: Anthony Hannant (LittleRedAnt)
Illustrator (step-by-steps): Kimberley Scott
Illustrator (incidentals and final crafts): Venetia Dean
Proofreader & Indexer: Sara Harper

Dewey categorisation: 531.1'1-dc23

ISBN 978 0 7502 8371 7

Printed in China

1 3 5 7 9 10 8 6 4 2

Wayland is a division of Hachette Children's Books,
an Hachette UK company.
www.hachette.co.uk

Picture acknowledgements:
All photographs: Shutterstock;
except: p. 13: Mark Williamson/Science Photo Library;
p. 15: NASA; p. 27: Phil Degginger/Alamy.

Contents

Zooooom!

What makes things zoom? What makes them whizz, slide, fall, crash or bump? The answer is forces. A force is a push or a pull that can make things move, stop or change shape.

SWING

ZOOOM!

GULP! Muscles in your throat squeeze hard to push food down into your stomach.

PLOP! If you throw a stone in a pond, your hand pushes it up, then gravity pulls it into the water.

LIKE WHAT?

There are forces at work all the time, all around you (and even inside you), making things happen. In fact, without these forces, nothing could happen at all!

You squeeze the bottle

It squirts paint out!

SQUEEEZE!

You force paint out of a tube by squishing the sides.

BOING! To jump on a trampoline, you push upwards with your legs.

Your legs push you up

Gravity pulls you down

Propeller pulls the plane forwards

WHEEEE! The force of gravity pulls you down a slide, or along a zipline.

Engine pushes the propeller around

VROOM! Engines burn fuel and turn wheels or propellers to make cars, buses and planes move.

WHOOOSH

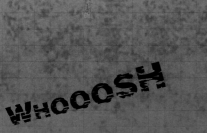

BEING A SCIENTIST

This book is full of exciting zooming, flying, sliding and squirting experiments to help you find out more about how forces work. When you're doing science experiments, be like a real scientist and remember these science tips:

1. Follow the instructions and always watch carefully to see what happens.

2. Write down your results in a notebook so you don't forget them.

3. Scientists often do experiments several times, to check they always work the same way.

Zooming cars

Use forces to make toy cars zoom, crash, jump and fly!

YOU WILL NEED
1) Several toy cars
2) Large, thin books or sheets of thick card
3) Toy bricks or small books
4) A large, hard floor space

Here's What to Do...

1. Push a car to see how far you can make it go.

2. Make a slope using card or a book, like this. Does it make the cars go? How?

3. Line up two cars opposite each other and crash them together.

4. Can you make a car do a daredevil leap over a row of other cars, then land safely?

WHAT'S GOING ON?

Making a car move in different ways uses different forces. You push a car using your hand. If you push it harder, you use more force, and it goes further.

If a car is at the top of a slope, the Earth's gravity pulls it down. Gravity is a pulling force between objects. The Earth's gravity is strong because the Earth has so much mass (it is so big and heavy).

When two cars crash, they push against each other. The pushes cancel each other out, stopping their movement.

! TROUBLESHOOTER

Push cars as straight as possible to stop them from skidding. If you have special toy car tracks, you can use them to set up slopes, crashes and jumps, too.

NEAR AND FAR

When you push a car with your hand, you have to touch it. This is a contact force. But some forces can work without touching, too. When your daredevil car is flying through the air, gravity still pulls it down. Gravity is a force at a distance – it can work even across empty space. Weird!

WHAT NEXT?

What happens if you crash marbles into each other? Can you control where they go?

Straw Shooter

Air can push to make things zoom!

YOU WILL NEED

1) An empty squeezy bottle with a narrow spout

2) Straws in two thicknesses – thin ones and slightly wider ones

3) Modelling clay

Here's What to Do...

1. Stick the thinner straw into the opening of the bottle and use modelling clay to seal it in place.

2. Take a wider straw and stick a small lump of modelling clay over the tip to make it airtight.

3. Slide the wider straw over the thinner straw sticking out of the bottle.

4. Pointing the shooter away from people and breakable objects, give it a hard squeeze!

WHAT'S GOING ON?

When you squeeze the bottle, you squeeze the air that's inside it. Some of the air zooms out through the thin straw and pushes against the modelling clay at the end of the wider straw, making it fly away.

! TROUBLESHOOTER

There should be no air gaps around the modelling clay – make sure it is sealed tightly.

Air is made of gas, meaning the tiny molecules in it float around freely. You can squeeze them together, but they will bounce back with a pushing force. That's why tyres and inflatables are bouncy. They have squashed or compressed air inside them that pushes outwards.

WHAT NEXT?

Experiment with how far you can shoot the straws.

Make a target to aim at, using a large cardboard box with holes cut in it. Mark each hole with a different score.

Heli~Spinner

When something pushes in one direction, there is an equal push back the other way. This is one way of making things lift off the ground.

Here's What to Do...

YOU WILL NEED
1) Lightweight card
2) Scissors
3) A hole punch
4) A straw (non-bendy if possible)
5) Sticky tape

1. Cut a piece of lightweight card 2 x 20 cm, and make a hole in the centre.

2. Make two cuts and folds in the card as shown here:

3. Wrap sticky tape around the top of the straw until it fits tightly into the hole in the card.

4. Spin the straw between your palms anti-clockwise, and let go.

WHAT'S GOING ON?

If it works, your heli-spinner should rise into the air. The cuts and folds in the card turn it into a set of rotor blades, like on a helicopter. As each blade pushes through the air, its angle and shape direct air downward. The air pushes back up, and this is what makes the spinner lift up and fly.

TROUBLESHOOTER

If the card won't stay in place firmly on the straw, use a bit more tape to keep it attached.

Aeroplane wings work in a similar way. As the plane moves forwards, the angle of the wings pushes air down. The air pushes back up, and the plane is lifted into the air.

Wing pushes air down

Air pushes wing up

WHAT NEXT?

Can you think of a way to make the straw spin faster at take-off?

Look for videos of real helicopters taking off. See if you can find seeds or other things that move through the air in a similar way.

Zero-gravity water squirt

What makes water squirt out of a leaky hole?
(This experiment is for outdoors!)

YOU WILL NEED
1) A water bottle
2) Water
3) A thick needle and an adult to help you

Here's What to Do...

1. Fill the bottle with water.

2. Ask an adult to make a small hole in the side, near the bottom, so that water can squirt out.

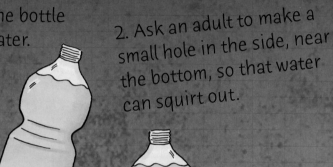

3. Refill the bottle, hold it up high, then drop it to the ground. Make sure no one's in the way!

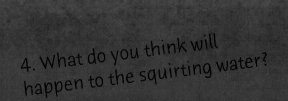

4. What do you think will happen to the squirting water?

WHAT'S GOING ON?

Gravity pulls down on the water and forces it out through the hole. When you drop the bottle, gravity pulls on the bottle as well as on the water, and they fall at the same speed. That means gravity can't pull the water out. While the bottle is falling, it's as if it is in zero gravity. When it lands, the water will start squirting out again.

SPACE SUCKER

Toilets flush using gravity, but in space that doesn't work, as nothing pulls the water, wee and poo down. Instead, space toilets have to use a sucking force to collect everything.

! TROUBLESHOOTER

As the bottle will fall quite fast, you have to watch very carefully to see what happens. If you have a video camera, you could film the experiment and play it back in slow motion.

VOMIT COMET

This plane, called the 'vomit comet' (because it makes you feel sick!), recreates low gravity by zooming downwards. The people inside fall at the same speed, and cannot feel the pull of gravity.

WHAT NEXT?

If you move the bottle upwards quickly instead, would that affect the squirt? Can you think of ways to make the squirt stronger or bigger?

Zooming balloon rocket

You'll be amazed how fast this balloon can zoom!

YOU WILL NEED

1) A balloon
2) A straw
3) A reel of strong sewing thread
4) Sticky tape

Here's What to Do...

1. Cut a piece of thread about 5 m long and thread the straw onto it.

2. Tie the thread tightly between two fixed objects, or just get two people to hold it stretched out.

3. Blow up the balloon, hold it closed, and sticky-tape it to the straw, like this.

4. Still holding the blown-up balloon closed, slide it along to the end of the thread, like this.

5. Five, four, three, two, one.... LET GO!

WHAT'S GOING ON?

When you let go of the balloon, the air inside comes shooting out, because it's being squeezed hard by the stretchy balloon skin. As the balloon pushes the air out, the air pushes back against the balloon, and the balloon and the straw get pushed forwards.

TROUBLESHOOTER

Taping the blown-up balloon to the straw while holding it closed can be tricky – it's easier if two people work together.

FORCES

This experiment shows that whenever there is a pushing force, there is also an equal pushing force in the opposite direction. The balloon pushes out the air – so the air pushes the balloon, making it zoom!

SPACE FORCES

Real rockets in outer space work this way. It doesn't matter that there is no air in space for them to push 'against'. As a rocket blasts out gases in one direction, it gets pushed in the other direction.

WHAT NEXT?

Can you make the balloon zoom upwards like a real rocket taking off? Does it work? When something moves upwards, it has to fight against the pulling force of gravity – so it might not go quite as fast.

Magazine tug-of-war

What mysterious force can stick two magazines together without using any glue?

YOU WILL NEED

Here's What to Do...

1) Two large magazines, paper pads or books with lots of pages – the thinner the pages, the better

1. Put the two magazines on a table with the edges of the pages facing each other, as above.

2. Now carefully interleave all the pages from both magazines, putting one on top of another in turn, as above.

3. Try pulling the magazines away from each other by their spines. If you can't do it, get two people to try, one pulling each magazine. Take care!

WHAT'S GOING ON?

You would think it would be easy to pull the magazines apart, but it's really hard! This is because of a force called friction. Friction makes surfaces grip onto each other and slow down as they rub past each other. Two sheets of paper rubbing together have some friction, but it's very weak. But when all the pages in the magazines are next to each other, there's so much friction that they grip onto each other very firmly.

! TROUBLESHOOTER

It works best if the magazines are roughly the same size.

FRICTION FIRE

Friction also heats objects up as they rub together. That's why rubbing sticks together can make fire! To test this, take two coins and hold them on a pad of paper with your fingertips. Keep one still and rub the other one to and fro very fast for 10 seconds. Does one get hotter?

WHAT NEXT?

Test the friction of different substances by seeing how easily they slide along a table top when pushed. Try a coin, piece of chocolate, a pebble, an eraser, and a plastic or wooden ruler. Which things grip best and which slide most easily?

Jelly slide

Friction is great if you want to get a good grip. But what if you don't? To reduce friction, you can use something slippery, such as oil.

Here's What to Do...

YOU WILL NEED

1) A pack of jelly
2) A smooth food tray or metal baking tray
3) A few books or a small box
4) Cooking oil such as sunflower oil

1. Break up the pack of jelly into cubes.

2. Make a slope by leaning the tray on the box or on a pile of books.

3. Put the jelly cubes on the slope and see if you can get them to slide down.

4. Cover the jelly and the slope in sunflower oil, and try again.

WHAT'S GOING ON?

For friction to work, two surfaces need to rub together. Without oil, tiny bumps and valleys on the surface of the jelly and tray catch and stick to each other. The oil acts as a barrier, separating those surfaces. Other liquids can also reduce friction. For example, it's easier to slip on a wet floor, because the water separates your feet from the floor, making it harder to grip.

! TROUBLESHOOTER

If you can't get or don't want to use jelly, cube or rectangle-shaped pencil erasers also work well.

SLIPPERY SKIS

Skiers and snowboarders rub wax on their skis or boards to reduce friction. Wax is thicker than oil and more solid, but still slippery. Because it's thicker, it's better at sticking to and staying on the skis or the board when zooming downhill.

WHAT NEXT?

Set up a jelly-cube downhill race using different liquids, such as cooking oil, water, milk and baby oil. Which reduces friction best?

flying bucket

When a cup full of water is upside down, the water will fall out. Won't it?

Here's What to Do...

YOU WILL NEED

1) A sturdy paper cup
2) Strong string
3) A large needle
4) Water
5) A safe open space outdoors

1. Ask an adult to help you make two holes at the sides of the cup, just below the rim.

Hole   Hole

2. Cut a 1 m long piece of string, put the ends into the holes, and tie them together as shown, making a mini-bucket with a long handle.

3. Half-fill your paper cup with water.

4. Carefully, outdoors and away from other people, swing the bucket to and fro, then right around in a circle, so it turns completely upside down.

WHAT'S GOING ON?

If you held your cup still and upside down, the force of gravity would pull the water out. But in this experiment, it doesn't!

When objects move, they keep going in the same direction, unless another force makes them change. As the water and cup whirl around, they are trying to keep going in a straight line, pulling away from you. But another force, the pull of the string, stops them from escaping, so they move in a circle instead. The two forces balance each other out, and the water stays in the cup.

! TROUBLESHOOTER

To make a stronger bucket, stack two cups together before you start.

PLANETS IN ORBIT

The same force holds the planets in place in our Solar System. They are moving fast and trying to go in a straight line. But the Sun's gravity pulls on them too, making them move in a circle, or orbit, around it. This fairground ride (see right) works in the same way.

WHAT NEXT?

How slowly can you whirl the cup around? Is it possible to let any water escape?

Whirling wind speed meter

Humans have invented all kinds of machines to measure forces. Here's one for measuring the pushing force of the wind.

Here's What to Do...

1. Use the pencil to make holes in the five paper cups as shown above.

2. Colour one of the cups with a marker to make it stand out from the others.

3. Thread two straws through the middle cup in a criss-cross shape.

A wind speed meter is called an anemometer.

4. Stick the pencil through the bottom of the cup with the eraser upwards.

5. Carefully stick the pin through the crossed straws and into the pencil eraser, like this:

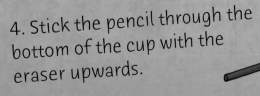

6. Attach the other four cups to the ends of the straws, like this, and hold in place with tape.

7. Stick the pencil point into a heavy lump of modelling clay, or into the ground.

8. When it's windy, see how fast your anemometer spins round!

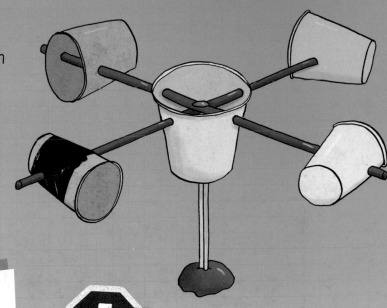

WHAT'S GOING ON?

As the wind blows, it pushes against the anemometer's cups. It flows more easily past the bottom end of each cup, but blows into the open ends, pushing them forward. As they are joined in the middle, they spin around. The faster the wind speed, the faster the anemometer spins.

! TROUBLESHOOTER

Don't push the pin down too hard – leave some space for the straws to spin.

Real anemometers at weather stations sometimes work like this too. The fastest wind ever recorded on Earth was a gust of 509 km/h (318 mph) inside a tornado in Oklahoma, USA.

WHAT NEXT?

Measure wind speed by counting how many times the coloured cup goes round in a minute.

Ping pong flinger

Machines use forces to do jobs for us. This ping pong flinger is based on the trebuchet – a weapon invented in medieval times for attacking castles, using the force of gravity.

YOU WILL NEED

1) A long wooden spoon
2) A pencil
3) An elastic band
4) Modelling clay
5) Books
6) Ping pong balls

1. Fix the wooden spoon and the pencil together in a criss-cross shape, by looping the elastic band around them in the middle several times.

2. Attach a large lump of modelling clay to the handle end of the spoon.

3. Make two piles of a few books of equal height and sit the pencil across the gap, with the spoon between the books.

4. Pull the bowl end of the spoon down to the ground and put a ping pong ball in it. When you let go, the trebuchet will fire.

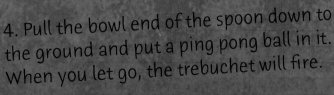

WHAT'S GOING ON?

A trebuchet is a type of lever – a long stick or beam with a balancing point, or pivot, in the middle. When you push one end down, the other end goes up, and vice versa. When you let go of the spoon, gravity pulls the heavy end down fast, making the bowl end jerk upwards. It pushes the ping pong ball into the air.

TROUBLESHOOTER

It will work best if the spoon has a deep, rounded bowl, not a flat one.

CASTLE ATTACK!

What did real trebuchets shoot at castles? Not ping pong balls, but heavy rocks, burning torches to start fires, dead animals, and even human heads! Yuck!

WHAT NEXT?

Experiment with different weights, spoons and heights to fire the balls as far or as high as possible. Make a target 'castle' out of a box and see if you can fire the balls inside.

Can you build a more permanent trebuchet model out of balsa wood or construction toys?

Gas-fuelled rocket

For this rocket, you need a container with a pop-off lid. Wear safety glasses and do this in an open space outside!

YOU WILL NEED

1) A plastic container with a pop-off lid
2) Plain card
3) Sticky tape
4) Felt-tip pens
5) Bicarbonate of soda, also called baking soda
6) A teaspoon
7) Vinegar
8) Tissues

Here's What to Do...

1. Roll a piece of card around your container and tape it in place to make a tube (the lid end of the container should be at the bottom).

2. Decorate your rocket with windows or numbers, and, if you like, a paper nose cone and fins.

3. Put a teaspoon of bicarbonate of soda into a square of tissue and wrap it up.

4. Holding the rocket pointing downwards and the container pointing up, half-fill it with vinegar.

5. Quickly drop in the tissue, press the lid on, turn it over, stand it on the ground and stand well back.

Baking soda

WHAT'S GOING ON?

Whoosh! If it works, your rocket will shoot up into the air as it fills with gas and the lid is forced off. The bicarbonate and vinegar create a chemical reaction that makes carbon dioxide gas. The gas fills up the container until it has such a strong pushing force that it blows the lid off.

TROUBLESHOOTER

If your rocket is too narrow to stand up easily, press it onto a modelling clay base.

WHAT NEXT?

Instead of vinegar, try other weak acids such as lemon juice, orange juice or fizzy water. Which works best?

To see the chemical reaction happen, mix the bicarbonate and acid in a bowl. You'll see the bubbles of gas that provide the pushing force.

Magnet power

Magnets have an amazing pulling and pushing force on each other and on some types of metal. Here are some experiments to try with them.

Here's What to Do...

1. Test magnets on different metal objects such as paperclips, pins, coins, hairclips, spoons, pans or your fridge. Which objects do the magnets stick to?

2. Use fine thread to attach metal paperclips to a surface, then use magnets to make them hover in mid-air.

3. Two magnets can push against each other if they are in the right position. Try positioning them so they push apart. Then give two people one of the magnets each and see if they can push them together.

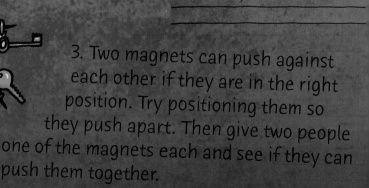

4. Do magnets work through paper, card, wood or your fingers?

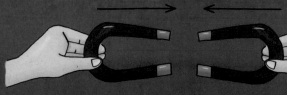

WHAT'S GOING ON?

What is a magnet? It's a piece of metal that creates a magnetic force field around it, which affects some types of metals and other magnets. Magnets can do this because the tiny particles in the metal are arranged in a particular pattern. Only some types of metals can become magnets. They include iron, steel (which contains iron) and nickel.

A magnet's two ends or sides are called its north and south poles. Two different poles will attract each other, while two alike poles will push apart, or repel, each other.

EVERYDAY MAGNETS

We use magnetic force for all kinds of things. Magnets hold up lists on fridges, sort out scrap metals, and make maglev trains (below) float above their tracks. They make credit card readers, speakers, microphones and motors work. The Earth is a giant magnet too, and the magnetic needle in a compass points to its North Pole.

WHAT NEXT?

Can you use magnets to set up a magic trick, making things seem to move by themselves?

Glossary

acid A type of chemical that can eat away at other materials if it is concentrated enough.

anemometer A machine for measuring wind speed.

compressed Squashed into a smaller space.

contact force A force that works on something it is touching.

energy The power to do work or make things happen.

force A push or pull that makes things move, stop or change shape.

force at a distance A force that works over a distance or empty space.

friction Gripping force between two surfaces that are rubbing together.

gas A substance in which molecules float around freely.

gravity A pulling force between objects.

lever A bar that can move up and down on a pivot, like a see-saw.

maglev A type of train that uses magnetic force to float above its track.

mass The amount of material an object contains, causing it to have weight.

molecules The tiny units that materials are made of.

orbit To circle around another object.

pivot A point that a lever or other machine part moves around.

poles The two ends or sides of a magnet.

repel To push away.

solar system Our Sun and the planets and moons that orbit around it.

trebuchet A medieval machine for shooting at castles.

further reading

BOOKS

Science Experiments That Fly and Move

by Kristi Lewandowski, Capstone Press, 2011

Heave! Forces and How They Move Things

by Peter Riley, Franklin Watts, 2012

The Flying Machine Book

by Bobby Mercer, Chicago Review Press, 2012

Amazing Science: Forces and Movement

by Sally Hewitt, Wayland, 2014

How Does Science Work: Forces and Movement

by Carol Ballard, Wayland, 2014

WEBSITES

Zoom Science: Forces

http://pbskids.org/zoom/activities/sci/#forcesenergy

ScienceKids: Forces in Action

http://www.sciencekids.co.nz/
gamesactivities/forcesinaction.html

Index